THE ESSENTIAL
CIGAR

THE ESSENTIAL
CIGAR

A Book for Connoisseurs

ANWER BATI

LORENZ BOOKS
NEW YORK • LONDON • SYDNEY • BATH

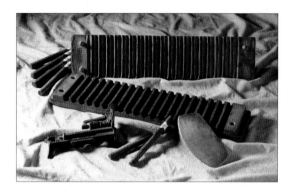

This edition first published in l997 by Lorenz Books
27 West 20th Street, New York, NY 10011

LORENZ BOOKS are available for bulk purchase for sales promotion and for premium use. For details, write or call
the sales director, Lorenz Books, 27 West 20th Street, New York, NY 10011; (800) 354-9657

Lorenz Books is an imprint of Anness Publishing Limited

ISBN 1 85967 461 5

Publisher: Joanna Lorenz
Project Editor: Fiona Eaton
Editorial Assistant: Emma Gray
Designer: Nigel Partridge
Photographers: Don Last, John Freeman

Printed and bound in Singapore

1 3 5 7 9 10 8 6 4 2

CONTENTS

INTRODUCTION

In the early days of World War II, the Prime Minister, Winston Churchill, received an urgent telephone call from the beleaguered manager of Dunhill, whose shop had just been bombed in a German air raid on London. The vital message was: "Your cigars are safe, Sir."

No doubt Churchill had many other things on his mind, but the story illustrates a number of traits of cigar lovers and their cigars. First, the importance of cigars to Winston Churchill. Second, the very strong preferences of serious cigar smokers for certain brands or types of cigar

(in Churchill's case always Hoyo de Monterrey double coronas) and loyalty to the shops that supply them. And last, the image that cigars, Havanas at least, have always had in the public imagination – a symbol of the powerful and wealthy.

Cigars are smoked slowly for relaxation and enjoyment or for their flavour and aroma during contemplative moments, and handmade cigars are attractive objects in their own right. In all this they differ from cigarettes, which are often smoked in moments of stress and are rarely appreciated for their taste or smell.

ABOVE: Winston Churchill with his wife and grandson.

LEFT: One of the first illustrations of smoking in a gentlemen's club in about 1814.

ABOVE: The portrait of Edward VII on this cigar box testifies to his love of smoking. Note the spelling of "segars".

Good cigars have distinctive qualities that depend on the precise blend of leaves, the skill of the maker, where the tobacco was grown and how it was fermented. In this, fine cigars are similar to fine wine, and, as a result, connoisseurs tend to be particular about which cigars they smoke, where they buy them and how they are stored. If you offer a machine-made cigar to a habitual smoker of Havana or Dominican cigars, the reaction might be similar to that of a lover of first-growth clarets when faced with Bulgarian plonk.

Because of the time needed to allow cigar tobacco to mature and the labour-intensive construction of handmade cigars, they are indeed expensive luxuries. Nor are good, well-stored cigars easy to come by. You can easily pay much more than the price of this book for a single cigar, so it is inevitable that most of the grander handmade brands are smoked by the relatively rich. But many people smoke the occasional handmade cigar after a fine meal, or to celebrate a special occasion. There is no need to be a buff, a tycoon or a regular smoker to enjoy a good cigar. This book has been written to enhance that enjoyment.

BELOW: A group of Russian artists smoking cigars, painted by Alexandre Guerassimov.

THE HISTORY OF CIGARS

Tobacco was probably first cultivated by the native Americans of the Yucatan peninsula in what is now Mexico, and the plant was later grown in both North and South America. We do not know when it was first grown, or smoked, but we can be pretty certain that the inhabitants of Europe were

unaware of tobacco until after Columbus's epic voyage of 1492.

Two of his sailors reported that the Cuban Indians smoked a primitive form of cigar, with twisted, dried tobacco leaves rolled in other leaves such as palm or plantain. In due course, Spanish and other European sailors caught the habit, as did the Conquistadors, and smoking spread to Spain and Portugal and eventually France, most probably through Jean Nicot, the French ambassador to Portugal, who gave his name to nicotine. Later, the habit spread to Italy and, after

Above: The first printed illustration of the use of the tobacco plant, dating from the 16th century.

Left: This cigar box illustration shows Columbus arriving in Cuba in 1492.

Opposite: An 18th-century French painting by Léonard Defrance showing a cigar factory.

ABOVE: This print dating from 1750 pictures tobacco being harvested. The crop is still harvested manually.

ABOVE: Sorting tobacco leaves after they have been cured in a factory, around 1750.

Sir Walter Raleigh's voyages to America, to Britain.

Smoking was familiar throughout Europe – in pipes in Britain – by the mid-16th century and, half a century later, tobacco started to be grown commercially in America.

Tobacco was originally thought to have medicinal qualities, but there were already some who considered it evil and it was denounced by Philip II of Spain, and James I of England.

The word cigar originated from *sikar,* the Mayan-Indian word for smoking,

which became *cigarro* in Spanish, although the word itself, and variations on it, did not come into general use until the mid-18th century.

Cigars, more or less in the form that we know them today, were first made in Spain in the early 18th century, using Cuban tobacco. At that time, no cigars were exported from Cuba. By 1790, cigar manufacture had spread north of the Pyrenees, with small factories being set

LEFT: Sir Walter Raleigh arriving in America. He took the smoking habit back to Britain.

up in France and Germany. The Dutch, too, started making cigars using tobacco from their Far Eastern colonies. But cigar smoking only became a widespread custom in France and Britain after the Peninsular War (1808–14), when returning British and French veterans made fashionable the habit they had learned while serving in Spain. Production of "segars" began in Britain in 1820, and in 1821 an Act of Parliament was needed to set out regulations governing their production. Because of an import tax, foreign cigars in Britain were already regarded as a luxury item.

Soon there was a demand for higher quality

cigars in Europe, and Spanish cigars were superseded by those made in Cuba, which was then a Spanish colony, where cigar production had started during the mid-18th century. Cigars, European smokers discovered, travelled better than tobacco.

The cigar probably arrived in North America in 1762, when Israel Putnam, later an American general in the American War of Independence (1774–1778), returned from Cuba, where he had served in the British army. He came back to his home in Connecticut, where tobacco had been grown by settlers since the 17th century, with a selection of Havana cigars and large amounts of Cuban tobacco seed. Cigar factories were later set up in the Connecticut area, processing the tobacco grown

ABOVE: An early 20th-century Dutch painting of a boy smoking a cigar. The Netherlands is a major producer of machine-made cigars.

LEFT: Enjoying a fine cigar isn't reserved for men only. There is a revival of smoking among women today.

ABOVE: In 1825, King Ferdinand VII of Spain encouraged the production of cigars in Cuba, then a Spanish colony.

from the Cuban seed. In the early 19th century American domestic production started to take off and Cuban cigars also began to be imported in significant numbers. But cigar smoking did not really boom in the United States until around the time of the Civil War in the 1860s, with individual brands emerging by the late 19th century. By then the cigar had become a status symbol in the United States.

During the same period, cigar smoking had become so popular among gentlemen in Britain and France that European trains introduced smoking cars to accommodate them, and hotels and clubs boasted smoking rooms. The after-dinner cigar, accompanied by glasses of port or brandy, also became a tradition. This ritual was given an added boost by the fact that the Prince of Wales, the future Edward VII and a leader of fashion, was a devotee, much to the annoyance of his mother, Queen Victoria, who disliked smoking.

Cigarettes, or paper cigars, first appeared on the scene in the early 19th century as a cheap alternative to cigars. The introduction of cigarette-making machines, in the 1880s, accelerated the growth in popularity of this form of smoking, which had become dominant by World War I.

As a response, the production of machine-made cigars began in Cuba in the 1920s, after which both the manufacture and smoking of handmade cigars fell into a slow but steady decline.

Smoking in general has, of course, become much less popular since the publication of the American Surgeon General's report on its effects on health in the early 1960s. But since the early 1990s, there has been a major revival in the popularity of handmade cigars: they have become chic once more, thanks to the enthusiasm shown for them by stars, such as Arnold Schwarzenegger, James Woods, Jack Nicholson, Sharon Stone, Demi Moore and model Linda Evangelista, demonstrating that, among the rich and famous, cigars are just as popular as ever.

ABOVE: *The French 19th-century poet Stephane Mallarmé, painted by François Nardi. Mallarmé was introduced to cigars by his father.*

LEFT: *The great British engineer Isambard Kingdom Brunel in front of the launching chains of the Great Eastern in 1857.*

WHERE CIGARS ARE MADE

Although its claims are sometimes disputed, Cuba remains the producer of the world's finest cigars, particularly those made from tobacco grown in the province of Pinar del Rio, at the western end of the island. The agricultural conditions of this region – rainfall, climate, and soil – are ideal for tobacco production, particularly in the Vuelta Abajo area, once described as a "natural humidor".

A number of Cuban cigar-makers emigrated to the United States during the mid-19th century, setting up factories in towns like Tampa and Key West in Florida. Later, many growers migrated to the Dominican Republic, Honduras and Mexico – the first two of which make cigars of high quality.

After Fidel Castro nationalized the Cuban cigar industry in the early 1960s, the Dominican Republic became the main base for the factory owners dispossessed by the communist regime, and now produces around half of all the handmade cigars imported into the United States.

Apart from Florida, the main American centre for cigar tobacco production is the Connecticut Valley, where conditions suitable for growing top quality cigar tobacco are created under huge tents.

Left: A tobacco crop in the Dominican Republic. Growing cigar tobacco is very labour intensive, with individual plants visited about 150 times each.

This area produces some of the world's best wrapper leaf, called Connecticut Shade, used in some of the finest Dominican cigars and for brands such as Macanudo from Jamaica, which has its own small cigar industry. There are also cigar industries, and cigar tobacco production, in Nicaragua, Brazil, Mexico and Ecuador.

The Americas and the Caribbean are not the only parts of the world where cigars are made and cigar tobacco grown. Sumatra and Java, formerly part of the Dutch East Indies, Africa (Cameroon wrapper leaves, grown from Cuban seed in subtropical West Africa, are of high quality), and the Philippines all produce tobacco and cigars.

ABOVE: An 18th-century print of Havana Harbour, as used on a cigar box.

BELOW: The Partagas factory in downtown Havana now also makes a number of other brands.

THE HAVANA CIGAR

To this day the romance of the cigar is very strongly based on the Havana, a national symbol of Cuba. With its perfect tobacco-growing conditions allied to the painstaking efforts of its cigar-makers, Cuba still produces the very best cigars available.

At the beginning of the 20th century, there were around 120 factories making over 200 different brands in Cuba and cigar-makers had become the core of the Cuban industrial working class.

After Fidel Castro's revolution against General Batista in 1959, the cigar industry, like much else,

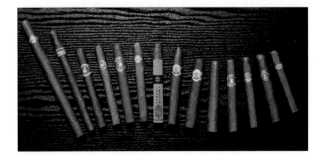

was nationalized, and the United States embargo on Cuba, imposed in 1962, meant that Havana cigars could no longer be exported to the United States.

Fidel Castro

Many claimed that the quality of Havana cigars fell after the revolution, but the Cubans responded by making first the Montecristo and then the Cohiba the world's most sought-after premium brands. Over the last few years, Cuba has exported between 50 and 80 million handmade cigars in 22 different brands annually – as against around 30 million just after the revolution.

LEFT: *Some of the best known Havana brands including Montecristo, Cohiba, Punch and Bolivar.*

OPPOSITE: *Cigar boxes including Cohiba, Bolivar, Partagas and the slide box of H. Upmann Connoisseur No. 1.*

THE DOMINICAN CIGAR AND OTHERS

*M*any fine cigars come from the Dominican Republic. In the past, Dominican growers have found it difficult to grow quality wrapper leaves (these are mainly imported from Connecticut in the United States) but recently they have had more success.

BELOW: Some Dominican brands, including Valdrych, Davidoff, Santa Damiana, Carlin and Don Diego.

RIGHT: Davidoff cigars have been made in the Dominican Republic since the early 1990s.

Some Dominican brands have the same names as Cuban ones (Partagas, Bolivar, and H. Upmann for instance); these are exported to the United

States. First class Dominican brands include Arturo Fuente, Avo, Casa Blanca, Davidoff, Dunhill and Paul Garmirian.

Fine handmade cigars, such as Don Ramos, Don Tomas, Excalibur, La Invicta and Zino, are made in Honduras. Nicaragua and a number of other Latin and South American countries also make cigars, but they are not, in the main, of comparable quality.

LEFT: *Don Tomas, one of the best-known Honduran brands.*

BELOW: *Cigars from Brazil, Nicaragua, Burma, the Philippines and Honduras.*

GROWING AND CURING TOBACCO

*M*aking good cigars is very similar to making good wine. Good wine depends on the type and quality of the grapes, the soil in which they are growing, the aspect of the vineyard and the weather conditions in each year. It also depends enormously on the skill of the winemaker and the process of fermentation. Making cigars has much in common with this process. The flavour and quality of a good cigar depends on the type of leaves used to make it, how

ABOVE: Wrapper leaf plants being attached to the muslin covers under which they are grown.

LEFT: Tobacco plants at the El Corojo plantation one week after planting.

ABOVE: Hanging wrapper leaves together in pairs in the curing barn.

long and well they are matured, the way they are allowed to ferment and finally the skill and expertise of the maker.

In Cuba, tobacco seedlings are transplanted from their shaded beds to the growing fields in late October. They are harvested four months later. Most of the plants are left exposed to the sun and the flower buds are removed as they appear, to prevent stunted growth. But plants which are destined to provide wrapper leaves for the very finest cigars are grown under muslin sheets. This keeps them smooth and prevents them from becoming too oily.

When the plants are harvested, leaves are removed by hand, using a single movement. It is a labour-intensive task: the leaves are cut in six stages, each phase taking around a week. Broadly speaking, the highest quality leaves are found in the middle, or *centro,* part of the plant, and are used as wrappers. The higher, or *corona,* leaves are used as fillers, and the lower leaves are used as binders.

The precise blend of these leaves, encased in an appropriate wrapper, is what makes a given cigar mild, medium or full-bodied.

ABOVE: Opening bundles of wrapper leaves so that they can be dampened before fermentation.

When the leaves have been picked the piles are strung up on horizontal poles and cured in large barns near the tobacco fields. There the heat and humidity are closely monitored as, over six to eight weeks, the green leaves turn to the familiar brown colour we associate with cigars.

Next the leaves go to a sorting house, where they are dampened, aired and then fermented in piles under jute coverings for up to three months to remove impurities such as ammonia. They are then graded for use as wrapper, filler or binder, and according to colour, size and quality. The sorted leaves then have a section of their mid-ribs stripped away. After that comes a further period of fermentation, between one and two months, depending on the type of leaf and its classification.

Finally, the leaves are sent in square bales to the factory or warehouse where they will mature further – in some cases for as long as two years, depending on which brand they are destined for.

The sheer time it takes to mature high quality tobacco leaf is not the least reason for the high prices premium cigars fetch. The care taken over maturing leaves properly is one of the key factors determining the quality of a cigar.

LEFT: The second fermentation takes place in large stacks. The temperature is carefully monitored throughout the process.

OPPOSITE: Wrapper leaves are hung to cure for up to 60 days. As chlorophyll turns to carotene the leaves brown.

CIGAR TOBACCO LEAVES

There are three parts to a handmade cigar: the wrapper leaf, the binder leaf, and the blend of filler leaves. Each has a specific role in the construction and smoking of a cigar.

The outside wrapper, the most expensive part of a cigar, determines the cigar's appearance. The leaf used for this purpose must be smooth, not too oily, and have a subtle bouquet. It also has to be pliable, to help smooth construction.

The binder leaf holds the filler

leaves inside the cigar together. It is normally a coarse leaf, usually from the upper part of the tobacco plant, and is chosen for its physical strength.

The leaves selected to make up the filler are arranged together in concertina fashion along their

LEFT: A flowering tobacco plant. In cultivation, the flower buds are removed as soon as they appear, to encourage fuller leaf growth, so a full bloom is rarely seen.

BELOW: A cross-section through a cigar. The binder leaves are coarse and strong.

length to form a series of passages through which air, and ultimately, of course, smoke, can be drawn. If you were to slice the cigar down its length, the arrangement of leaves inside the binder would resemble the pages of a book.

Three different types of leaf are normally used for the filler: dark, strongly flavoured and slow-burning *ligero* leaves from the top of the tobacco plant are placed in the middle of the filler. These

RIGHT: The leaves undergo vigorous inspections at all stages of production. These wrapper leaves are being checked during primary fermentation.

BELOW: A wrapper leaf. It must be smooth and unblemished.

are surrounded by lighter, milder *seco* leaves from the middle of the tobacco plant. *Volado* leaves from the bottom of the plant are usually placed on the outside of the filler section because of their good burning qualities.

The relative proportions of these three types of leaf in the filler are the key to the flavour of a cigar, and cigar-makers aim to keep these proportions consistent for each size within any given brand.

HOW HAVANA CIGARS ARE MADE

Havanas today are made in much the same way they have been for the past 150 years. There are seven production stages. Two to four filler leaves – the number depends on the size and blend – are rolled into two half-binder leaves. The filler leaves must be evenly distributed, otherwise the cigar will not draw easily. If it is too loosely filled, it will burn too fast and become hot and acrid. The flavour and draw of a cigar must remain consistent for a particular brand, so the selection of filler leaves is vital.

This "bunch", as it is known, is now placed into a wooden mould of the appropriate size for the cigar being made. The surplus filler is trimmed from

BELOW: Arranging filler leaves to be rolled in the binder. The blend of filler leaves gives the cigar its flavour and strength.

BELOW: Rolling the blend of filler leaves in the binder leaves to make a "bunch".

LEFT: *After the bunches are pressed to the correct shape and trimmed to the right length, they are ready to have wrapper leaves rolled around them. The moulds are usually wooden.*

BELOW: *The wrapper leaf is carefully stretched and then rolled around the bunch.*

the ends of the bunch. The mould is pressed.

When the bunch is ready, the third stage is to trim the selected wrapper leaf to the correct size. For this, an oval steel cutter, called a *chaveta, is* used.

The bunch is arranged across the trimmed wrapper at an angle and rolled from one end. The wrapper is gently stretched and wound around the

bunch, with each turn overlapping. When the rolling is complete, the end is stuck down with a drop of flavourless vegetable gum.

The cigar is then rolled under the flat blade of the *chaveta* to ensure that it has been evenly made.

ABOVE: A typical Havana cigar maker's work bench with a chaveta *in the foreground.*

OPPOSITE: After being rolled, cigars are tied in bundles of 50 and are treated for pests in a vacuum fumigator. They are then stored in cool cabinets to allow them to lose excess moisture.

LEFT: A circular piece of left-over wrapper leaf is cut out to provide the cap – which is gummed on.

A small, round piece of wrapper leaf is then cut out to form a cap, which is stuck in place using the colourless gum. In the making of some of the most expensive cigars, the wrapper itself is used to form the cap. In the final process, the open end of the cigar is guillotined to the correct length. They are then stacked in loosely tied bundles of 50.

Once the cigars are made, a percentage from each roller undergo rigorous quality control. A cigar is tested in terms of construction, size, girth, how evenly it burns, draw, flavour and many other factors. Two hundred rollers at the Partagas factory in central Havana make around five million cigars a year, the majority for export. A quality product is expected and this is tested for at this stage.

While a sample of cigars are being tested, the rest are treated for potential pests. The cigars are then stored, still in their bundles of 50, in refrigerated

LEFT: A skilled cigar-maker can roll an average of 100 medium-sized cigars a day, but the very fastest rollers can almost double this amount.

cabinets for a couple of weeks to allow them to lose excess moisture.

Next they are sorted according to their colour (there are as many as 60 possible shades).

Finally they have labels put on them and are packed into cedar boxes, with each box containing cigars of the same shade. The boxes are sealed.

The broad stages of production described here apply to all handmade cigars, although there may, of course, be subtle variations in procedure between different factories and countries.

ABOVE: Labels are attached to Dunhill cigars in the Dominican Republic.

BELOW: The finished cigars are grouped by colour before being packed. This is a skilled job, since there are about 60 subtle shades of wrapper leaf.

BELOW: Packing labelled cigars of the same shade in their cedar boxes. Each box is labelled and sealed as proof of its authenticity.

THE STRUCTURE OF A CIGAR

Generally speaking, it is easy enough to tell the difference between most machine-made cigars and handmade cigars. Machine-made cigars are cheaper, there is no cap at one end and they are usually sold in small sizes.

There are, however, more expensive machine-made cigars, some of them bearing famous brand

RIGHT: Checking the length of a Cohiba lancero.

names and packaged like their handmade counter-parts, which can be harder to tell apart from handmade cigars.

The key difference between the two becomes obvious only when the cigar is cut open. Handmade cigars use long fillers – leaves that run the whole length of the cigar. This means that they burn more slowly and evenly than machine-made ones, which are normally made with threads of filler leaf.

Another difference is that, with the exception of the most expensive brands, the wrapper leaves on

LEFT: Filler leaves being folded into one another. They will run the length of the cigar.

machine-made cigars are not usually as smooth, unblemished or carefully matured as those on hand-made ones.

The more expensive machine-made brands are made using individual binder leaves, but most mass-market brands are made rather in the same way as cigarettes, using scraps of filler leaf compressed into shape, with continuous sheets of processed binder

ABOVE: A handmade cigar. TOP: with wrapper. MIDDLE: without wrapper. BOTTOM: the filler with the binder removed.

and wrapper leaves wound around them. They are then cut to length.

The connoisseur can contrast this with the skill that goes into rolling a handmade cigar, and the time and care involved in making sure that all the leaves are properly selected and matured.

THE SIZE RANGE

Surprisingly, when a tycoon lights up a fat cigar, it is not simply a matter of showing off: the fatter a cigar is, the fuller flavoured it tends to be, and the slower and more smoothly it smokes. Apart from the fact that filler leaves can be more subtly blended in bigger cigars, it is worth noting that the largest cigars are made by the most skilled rollers.

There are as many as sixty cigar sizes. The sizes often have the same names but the exact dimensions vary from brand to brand.

The thickness of a cigar is referred to in terms of its *ring gauge,* which is expressed in measures of $\frac{1}{64}$ in (0.4 mm). So, if a cigar has a ring gauge of 32, it is $\frac{32}{64}$ or $\frac{1}{2}$ in

Size	Length (inches)	Length (mm)	Ring Gauge
Double Corona	7⅞	200	49
Churchill	7	178	47
Robusto	5	127	50
Lonsdale	6½	165	42
Corona	5½	140	42
Petit Corona	5	127	42

(12.5 mm) thick; and were a cigar to have a ring gauge of 64, it would be 1 in (25.4 mm) thick.

Although they might have a favourite brand or size, many seasoned smokers vary their choice depending on the time of day. Smaller, lighter cigars are smoked before lunch and a big, full-bodied cigar after a heavy dinner. If time is at a premium, experienced smokers might go for the robusto size – a short but punchy cigar.

OPPOSITE PAGE: Petit Corona (Punch Petit Corona). ABOVE, LEFT TO RIGHT: Robusto (Partegas Series D. 4), Corona (Montecristo No. 3), Lonsdale (Bolivar Lonsdale), Churchill (Romeo Y Julieta Churchill), Double Corona (Hoyo de Monterrey).

THE COLOUR RANGE

Cigar wrappers are normally classified accord-ing to seven basic colours, but they can come in many different shades.

Generally speaking, cigars described as *claro* have pale wrappers and are mild. Those called *colorado* are darker, stronger and matured longer. *Maduro* wrappers are a very dark brown, and *oscuro* wrap-pers, which are rare today, are almost black.

BELOW: Havana cigars are sorted into over 60 different shades before being packed into boxes.

ABOVE: The cigars in a box should all be an even colour.

OPPOSITE: Cigar colour from the dark brown maduro *at the very top, reddish* colorados, *and* claro *shades further down.*

CHOOSING A CIGAR

*I*f you are choosing a cigar there are a few rules worth observing.

• If you can, always try to look inside any box of cigars that you are thinking of buying. Then check the following:

• They all should be more or less of the same colour. As a general (but not invariable) rule, the darker a cigar, the fuller bodied and sweeter it is likely to be.

• Make sure that the wrapper leaves have a nice sheen and that none of them are damaged.

• The cigar should not be dry or brittle. Feel a couple of the cigars: they should be smooth and firm but give slightly when you press gently between finger and thumb.

• Smell a cigar or two: see if you like the bouquet. It should be distinct. If you can't smell anything, don't buy them.

• Select a cigar to suit your needs. Novice smokers are advised to start with smaller cigars, for example the half corona size, normally around 127 mm (5 in) long, with a ring gauge of 42. Smaller cigars are also better suited for daytime smoking.

LEFT: Feeling a cigar. It should give a little but should spring back into shape.

OPPOSITE: Ask to see the open box of cigars before buying them. The wrappers should have a lovely sheen to them, as on these Honduran Hoyo de Monterrey cigars.

THE CIGAR BOX

The practice of packing cigars in cedar boxes goes back to 1830, when the bank of H. Upmann decided to send cigars to its senior staff in London in boxes similar to the ones we are familiar with today. Each box bore the bank's symbol. The bank eventually decided to diversify into the cigar business, and, in time, other Havana brands and most other hand-made cigar-makers followed the Upmann example. The choice of cedar wood wasn't accidental: enclosing cigars in cedar helps to keep them moist and allows them to mature.

ABOVE: The green Cuban seal guarantees authenticity.

LEFT: The "Habanos" logo has been used on Cuban cigar boxes since 1994.

RIGHT: The Ramon Allones brand, founded in 1837, was the first to use coloured, decorative brand labels.

The idea of branding cigars started at around the same time, as the industry grew and rudimentary marketing became important to differentiate between manufacturers. As a result, cigar boxes began to be decorated with colourful labels bearing the brand name and became attractive objects in their own right. From

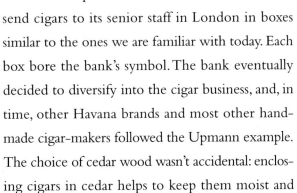

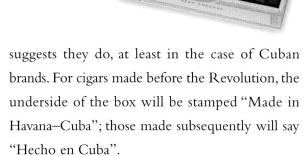

1912 onwards, Havana cigar boxes were also sealed with a green printed label to guarantee authenticity. This custom was soon emulated by almost all other handmade cigar makers.

It is well worth studying the bottom of any box of cigars you are thinking of buying, in the same way as you would a wine label, unless you are dealing with a shop you know well. First, you need to be certain that the cigars come from where the box

RIGHT: A box of H. Upmann cigars. The company, originally a bank, was the first to package cigars in cedar boxes.

suggests they do, at least in the case of Cuban brands. For cigars made before the Revolution, the underside of the box will be stamped "Made in Havana–Cuba"; those made subsequently will say "Hecho en Cuba".

The key thing, however, is to ensure that the cigars are indeed handmade. The box must state "Totalmente a mano" – as Havana boxes have since 1989. The same applies to non-Havana cigar brands. Make sure that the box says "Handmade".

LEFT: Don Diego cigars from the Dominican Republic.

RIGHT: The bottom of a current Cuban cigar box. Check that it says "hecho en Cuba" and "totalmente a mano" to ensure that the cigars are genuine and handmade.

THE CIGAR BAND

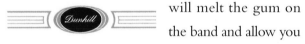

The cigar band, once ornate but now often simple, was introduced by Gustave Bock, a cigar manufacturer of Dutch origin, in the mid–19th century. Bands followed boxes and labels as yet another method of branding cigars. Some brands, such as the Cuban Romeo Y Julieta, use more than one band design. The brand's Churchill size has a gold band, whereas all its other sizes have red ones.

Whether you should smoke a cigar with the band on or off is entirely up to you, although, in Britain, it used to be considered "bad form" to show the brand you were smoking. If you prefer to smoke a cigar without its band, do not remove it until you have smoked it for a minute or two. That way, the heat will melt the gum on the band and allow you to take it off without damaging the wrapper leaf.

LEFT: *The trend today for cigar bands is towards simplicity.*

RIGHT: *Three Havana brands: Punch, created for the British market in 1904, was named after the popular magazine of the time; Bolivar is named after the 19th-century revolutionary, and Romeo Y Julieta was the favourite story of the cigar rollers.*

CUTTING THE CAP

*A*ll handmade cigars, and some of the more expensive machine-made brands, have a closed end covered by a cap. For many people, cigar smoking is a ritual activity, and there is no more important part of the ritual than cutting the cigar. This end needs to be cleanly and levelly cut around 3 mm (⅛ in) above the base of the cap.

But the method you use for this is a matter of personal choice. You can use a special cigar cutter or you can just as easily use a sharp knife or even your fingernails if you are skilled enough, in which case, simply pinch off the top of the cap.

There are a large number of cutters on the market, ranging from small, cheap, easily portable plastic guillotines to much fancier versions, small, decorative works of art in their own right, made of steel, gold, silver and enamel. Guillotines come in single or double-bladed versions, but the latter is the best tool for the job. There are also a number of cigar scissors available

ABOVE: Cigar cutters can be very stylish objects. This round, single guillotine type is one of the easiest to use.

LEFT: Cutting the cap is an essential part of the cigar smoking ritual.

that, although attractive, can be cumbersome in the wrong hands and need some skill to use properly. Other cutters make a wedge shape in the cap, or pierce it.

Whichever type of cutter you use, make sure it is sharp. Do not pierce the cap, as some people still do; it will make the cigar overheat by compressing the vital filler leaves and can completely ruin the flavour of the cigar.

RIGHT: Cigar cutters come in a huge range of styles.

ABOVE: Professionals in cigar shops often use cigar scissors, but they take a little mastering.

Do make sure you cut the cap carefully. If you don't, it will seriously impair your enjoyment of your cigar. If the cut isn't level the cigar's draw will be affected, and it will heat up unevenly. Ensure that the wrapper leaf is not damaged, and whatever you do, don't cut below the level of the cap, since this will almost surely risk damaging the wrapper. Do not blow through a cigar before lighting since this injects moisture into the cigar.

LIGHTING A CIGAR

*L*ighting a cigar is not merely a matter of applying a flame to it: a well and carefully lit cigar will always be more enjoyable than one that is badly lit.

It doesn't matter whether you use a match or a lighter, although a lighter should burn butane rather than gasoline. Most major cigar shops supply long, slow-burning matches that do the job very well, but you can just as easily use an ordinary match, providing it is not too sulphurous or waxy. The important thing is that the cigar is evenly lit and that its flavour isn't conta–minated by the source of the

ABOVE: Cigar matches are long and slow burning.

ABOVE RIGHT: Hold the end of the cigar in the flame and make sure it is evenly charred.

RIGHT: Draw slowly on the cigar while gradually rotating it.

flame, which is a good reason for avoiding candles.

Make sure you have a decent-sized flame. Hold the cigar horizontally, with the flame just touching it. Then slowly revolve the cigar until the end is evenly charred.

Hold the flame about half an inch away from the end and draw slowly on the cigar, keeping it horizontal and continuing to turn it. The end of the cigar should now ignite.

Gently blow on the glowing end to ensure that it is burning evenly. This is important, otherwise one side will burn faster than the other, which will affect the flavour and draw of the cigar and increase

BELOW: This cartoon strip from 1874 depicts a young boy's first encounter with a cigar!

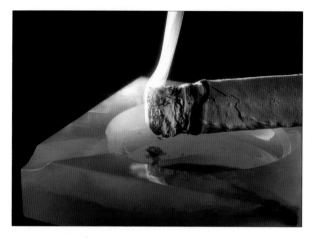

ABOVE: You can always relight your cigar if it goes out – but don't leave it more than a couple of hours.

the likelihood of the cigar going out.

The key to maximum enjoyment of a cigar, once it has been properly lit, is to avoid overheating the filler. So smoke slowly, without puffing too much on the cigar or dragging on it.

If your cigar goes out, as it might well, tap away any ash, relight it as before, and blow through it to remove any stale smoke before you start smoking again. But beware that relighting a cigar after more than a couple of hours will almost certainly mean that its flavour is significantly impaired.

STORING CIGARS

Cigars are a natural, organic product and need to be stored just as carefully as you might store food or wine.

The air-conditioned or centrally heated home is their biggest enemy: cigars should ideally be kept in a humid environment, avoiding too much heat or cold. Really serious cigar smokers entrust their reserve of cigars to the care of their favourite cigar merchant, while others have specially adapted cellars or closets in their homes for the purpose. But there are much simpler, practical measures that anybody can take.

The key to storing cigars properly is to make sure they don't dry out. So keep them (in their cedar boxes) in an airtight cupboard or box, away from heat sources. It helps to keep a damp sponge in the cupboard and to check from time to time that it hasn't dried out. If you have only a few cigars, put the box they come in into a sealed polythene bag, having sprayed the inside of the bag with a little water.

ABOVE: A special tin box of Dunhill cigars issued to servicemen during World War II.

LEFT: Slimline, desk top humidors are convenient for storing a few cigars.

You could, of course get a humidor, a special container for keeping cigars moist. These range from small ones, made of wood or leather and intended to be used when travelling, to major pieces of furniture.

Humidors were traditionally made of wood such as walnut, mahogany and rosewood, but there are also plastic models on the market today.

It is important that a humidor is well-made, unvarnished inside and, above all, that it has a heavy, tight-fitting lid. Remember that whatever humidification system it uses, from a sponge to chemicals, you cannot just go away and forget it: the system will need to be topped up from time to time.

Cigars in aluminium tubes lined with cedar, though very convenient to carry, can sometimes become rather dry as the tubes are not completely airtight. If cigars are wrapped in cellophane, they are best left in their wrappings unless you have a

ABOVE: You can carry cigars in a sealable polythene bag: most good cigar shops will package loose cigars this way.

LEFT: A wide range of humidors is available in different styles, sizes and price ranges.

RIGHT: Some humidors are fancy pieces of furniture as well as storage boxes for cigars.

trustworthy humidor in which to transfer them swiftly.

Because of the importance of storing cigars properly, when you buy cigars from anywhere other than a major cigar shop, do make sure you always check that they aren't just kept on a shelf or in a cupboard: you're pretty sure to be disappointed in your purchase if they are.

ABOVE: *This sort of "tele-scopic" case is one of the best to carry cigars in.*

ABOVE: *Keep your cigars in their cedar boxes unless you have a humidor.*

LEFT: *A simple humidor with a meter to show humidity. The divider keeps the different flavoured cigars separate.*

RIGHT: *Metal tubes (lined with cedar) are convenient for travelling.*

OPPOSITE: *The cigar storeroom at Dunhill in London keeps the cigars at perfect humidity.*

WHERE TO BUY CIGARS

Visiting one of the world's great cigar stores, such as Davidoff, Dunhill or Robert Lewis in London, Nat Sherman in New York, or La Civette in Paris, is more than just a matter of shopping. For the devoted cigar smoker, it is to enter a world dedicated to one of your main pleasures, full of cheering sights and smells, all of them redolent of calm and relaxation.

London is probably the best, though not the

ABOVE: Engraving of a German tobacco shop, 1850.

LEFT: The maturing room at Dunhill in London, dating from 1928. Some of the larger cupboards can hold in the region of 30,000 cigars.

OPPOSITE: The Dunhill shop in Duke Street, London.

LEFT: Frederick Tranter in Bath, England is one of the smallest cigar shops of good repute.

BELOW: A selection of cigars at the Havana Club in London's Knightsbridge.

cheapest, place in Europe to buy good handmade cigars, closely followed by Geneva and Paris. There are, of course, fine cigars to be found in the best American shops but, alas, because of the trade embargo, no Havanas.

You can trust the great cigar shops, but if you venture to outfits without knowing their reputation, it is worth being a little more cautious. Be careful when you are tempted by sale bargains or duty-free cigars at the airport: make sure you are not being sold machine-made cigars with famous

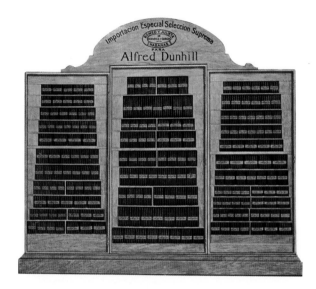

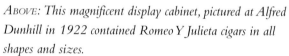

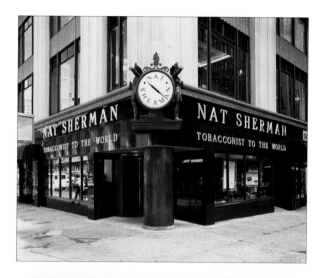

ABOVE: This magnificent display cabinet, pictured at Alfred Dunhill in 1922 contained Romeo Y Julieta cigars in all shapes and sizes.

ABOVE RIGHT AND RIGHT: The Nat Sherman shop in New York: one of the best and most famous cigar stores in the United States.

labels by checking the bottom of the box.

And, if you can, always try to look inside any box of cigars you are thinking of buying. If possible, buy cigars in boxes of 10 or 25 rather than as singles or boxes of five. The larger packs are reputed to be of slightly better quality.

SOME GREAT CIGARS

This is the author's personal selection of some of the world's best and most famous cigars. An appreciation of flavour and aroma are, of course, a matter of personal taste, but a little guidance may be useful if you are new to buying premium cigars. Try a number of different cigar brands in a variety of flavours, strengths and sizes to find a cigar that you really enjoy.

OPUS X
*This Dominican cigar, with its beautiful oily wrapper, has
a nutty flavour and draws well.*

BOLIVAR *(Belicosas Finos)*
*A very full-bodied Cuban favourite. The thing to go for after
a heavy dinner.*

COHIBA *(Lancero)*

*Cohiba is the world's most expensive brand, and the lancero
— with its characteristic cap — is one of its best-known sizes.*

DAVIDOFF *(Double R)*

*Cigars bearing the great Davidoff brand used to be made in
Cuba. Now they come from the Dominican Republic. This
double corona is one of the most recent to join the range.*

DUNHILL *(Peravias)*

*A rich, elegant cigar, aged before it is distributed, made in the
Dominican Republic for the grand old firm of Dunhill.*

EXCALIBUR No II
*An excellent, well-made, medium-bodied cigar made in
Honduras.*

HOYO DE MONTERREY *(Double Corona)*
*Beautifully blended and subtle for its size, this cigar is a
favourite of connoisseurs.*

MONTECRISTO A
*ABOVE: A giant Cuban cigar beloved of show business folk
with giant personalities.*

MACANUDO *(Vintage No 1)*
*OPPOSITE: Made in Jamaica with Dominican filler and
Connecticut wrapper. Not cheap, but a fine, mild cigar. Perfect
for daytime smoking.*

PARTAGAS *(Series D No 4)*
ABOVE: A powerful cigar, characteristic of one of Cuba's oldest and most full-bodied brands.

PAUL GARMIRIAN *(Lonsdale)*
BELOW: A brand founded by the eponymous connoisseur in 1991. Very well made, rich but subtle.

PUNCH *(Punch)*
BELOW: A famous Havana name. A medium-bodied corona, though with a bigger ring gauge than usual.

SAINT LUIS REY *(Regios)*
OPPOSITE: Havanas don't come much better if you like a full-bodied, aromatic cigar.

ROMEO Y JULIETA *(Churchill)*
BELOW: Romeo Y Julieta was the first brand to name a cigar after the great statesman.

THE DIRECTORY

UNITED KINGDOM

LONDON

Alfred Dunhill of London
30 Duke Street, London SW1Y
Tel: 0171 499 9566

Davidoff of London
35 St James's Street, London SW1A
Tel: 0171 930 3079

Harrods Cigar Room
Knightsbridge, London SW1X
Tel: 0171 730 1234

The Havana Club
165 Sloane Street, London SW1X
Tel: 0171 245 0890

J.J. Fox of St James
19 St James's Street, London SW1A
Tel: 0171 930 3787

Sautter of Mayfair
106 Mount Street, London W1Y
Tel: 0171 499 4866

The Segar and Snuff Parlour
27a The Market, Covent Garden,
London WC2
Tel: 0171 836 8345

Selfridges
400 Oxford Street, London W1A
Tel: 0171 529 1234

Shervingtons
337 High Holborn, London WC1V
Tel: 0171 405 2929

Walter Thurgood
161-162 Salisbury House,
London Wall, EC2M
Tel: 0171 528 5437

Wards of Gresham Street
60 Gresham Street, London EC2V
Tel: 0171 606 4318

OUTSIDE LONDON

Frederick Tranter
5 Church Street, Abbey Green, Bath
Tel: 01225 466197

Gauntleys of Nottingham
4 High Street, Nottingham
Tel: 01159 417973

Harrison & Simmonds
17 St John's Street, Cambridge
Tel: 01223 324515

Herbert Love
31 Queensferry Street, Edinburgh
Tel: 0131 225 8082

John Hollingsworth & Son Limited
5 Temple Row, Birmingham
Tel: 0121 235 7768

Lands (Tobacconists) Ltd
29 Central Chambers, Henley Street,
Stratford-upon-Avon
Tel: 01789 292508

Tobacco World (Cheltenham)
Regent Arcade, Cheltenham
Tel: 01242 222037

Tobacco World of Chester
78 Northgate Street, Chester
Tel: 01244 348821

UNITED STATES

NEW YORK

Arnold's Cigar Store
323 Madison Avenue, New York, NY
Tel: 212 697 1477

Davidoff of Geneva
535 Madison Avenue
54th Street, New York, NY
Tel: 212 751 9060

De La Concha Tobacconists
1390 Avenue of the Americas
New York, NY
Tel: 212 757 3167

Nat Sherman Inc.
500 Fifth Avenue, New York, NY
Tel: 212 246 5500

North Cigar Lounge
483 Columbus Avenue, New York, NY
Tel: 212 595 5033

OUTSIDE NEW YORK
Diebels Sportsmens Gallery
426 Ward Parkway, Kansas City, KS
Tel: 800 305 2988

Georgetown Tobacco
3144 M North West, Washington DC
Tel: 202 338 5100

Holt Cigar Co. Inc.
1522 Walnut Street, Philadelphia, PA
Tel: 800 523 1641

The Humidor Inc.
6900 San Pedro Avenue, San Antonio, TX
Tel: 210 824 1209

Jack Schwartz Importers
175 W. Jackson, Chicago, IL
Tel: 312 782 7898

J.R. Tobacco of America Inc.
I-95 at Route 70, Selma, AL
Tel: 800 572 4427

The Owl Shop
268 College Street, New Haven, CT
Tel: 203 624 3250

The Pipe Squire
346 Coddrington Center
Santa Rosa, CA
Tel: 707 573 8544

Rich Cigar Store Inc.
801 Southwest Alder St, Portland, OR
Tel: 800 669 1527

Tinder Box Santa Monica
2729 Wilshire Boulevard
Santa Monica, CA
Tel: 310 828 4511

AUSTRALIA

MELBOURNE

Alexander's Cigar Divan
at Crown Towers
8 Whiteman Street, Southbank
Tel: (03) 9292 7842 Fax: (03) 9292 7851

Baranow's Fine Cigars
P.O. Box 29, Preston vic 3072
Tel: (03) 9479 6579 Fax (03) 9478 6549
E-mail: Cigar1 @ MSN.com
Web site: HTTP://WWW.aml.com.
au/Cigar1.htm

Benjamin's Fine Tobacco
Shop 10, Strand Central
250 Elizabeth Street
Tel: (03) 9663 2879 Fax: (03) 9663 2181
E-mail: Bentob @ Netspace.net.au

SYDNEY

Alexander's Cigar Divan
at Pierpont's, Hotel Intercontinental
117 Macquarie Street
Tel: (02) 9252 0280

Sol Levy
713 George Street
Tel: (02) 9211 5628

ADELAIDE

Tunney's
38-40 Grote Street
Tel: (08) 8231 5720

INDEX & ACKNOWLEDGEMENTS

ACKNOWLEDGEMENTS

The publishers would like to thank the following people and organizations for supplying additional pictures for this book: AKG p 52r *The Finest Sort,* an engraving by Stahlstich von Brennhäuser after the painting by Hano von Rohmberg: Bridgeman Art Library pp 7br *Portrait of the Artists Ivan Pavlov, Vassili Bakcheiev, Vitold Bialynitski-Biroulia and Vassili* by Alexandre Guerassimov, Tretyakof Gallery, Moscow; 12 *King Ferdinand VII* by Francisco Jose de Goya Y Lucientes; 13bl Isambard Kingdom Brunel, 1857, photograph by Robert Howlett, Stapleton Collection; 13r *Portrait of Stephane Mallarmé* by François Nardi: Dunhill pp 6, 14, 24t, 31tr, 31bl, 31br, 44t, 48t, 49bl, 51, 52bl, 53, 55tl: John Hall p 7tl: Magnum p 16 Castro, End of Era by Bob Henriques: Mary Evans Picture Library pp 8t; 11t *A Small Dutch Boy with a Big Dutch Cigar* by Nico Jungmann; 47b *Our First Cigar,* 1874, by T de Witt Talmadge: Nat Sherman Inc. pp 55tr, 55 br, 63br: Richard Tranter p 54l: Visual Arts Library p 9 *A Visit to the Tobacco Factory* by Léonard Defrance, Liège Museum of Art: Jon Wyand pp 1, 15, 20l, 20r, 21, 22l, 22r, 23, 25l, 25r, 26l, 26r, 27l, 27r, 28, 29, 30tl, 30tr, 30b, 32l, 32r, 36l. l=left, r=right, b=bottom, t=top

The publishers would also like to thank Jerry Gough and Neil Millington of The Havana Club, London, Alfred Dunhill Ltd, Desmond Sautter Ltd, Forrestal (Cigars) Ltd, Ron Grace, John Hall, Hunters & Frankau, London Cigar Company, Lorretta Cigars (London) Ltd, Premium Cigar Ltd, Rothmans International, Sahakian-Davidoff, N. R. Silverstone, G. Smith & Sons, The Snuff Centre, Tor Imports and Valdrych SA.